AF584246

DOG

DOG

SHAUN TAN

Once we were strangers,
legs bent the wrong way,
rough voices falling to the wind,
every tooth and claw and stick a weapon,
every urge a ragged mystery.

But we always wanted more than this.
In our hearts we knew there was more.

One day I threw my stick at you.
You brought it back.
My hand touched your ear.
Your nose touched the back of my knee.
Then we were walking side by side
as if it had always been this way.

Time flowed out before us,
an endless river,
the plains opened up, the sky lifted
and you cried out to me then,
This world is ours!
And so it was.

When I ran, you ran.
When you called, I answered.
Together we chased all loneliness and fear,
and saw everything happen
that was ever going to happen.
Every beauty and terror, every rise and fall.

And when you died
I took you down to the river.
And when I died
you waited for me by the shore.

So it was that time passed between us.

And then, somehow, we were together again.
This is how it's always been.

But now everything is different.
The river flows wrongly,
the plains are gone,
the sky presses down like a thousand ceilings.
It feels like time is only ever running away from us.
Where will we go? What will we do?

You pull at my hand,
push your nose to the back of my knee,
and cry out to me as you always do,
This world is ours!
And just like that
we are walking again.

Afterword

The relationship between dogs and humans is unlike that of any other. There are perhaps few inter-species friendships so epic and transforming, spanning some 15,000 years, enduring the vagaries of history, the rise and fall of countless societies, shaping each in turn. Every time I see people walking their dogs at my local park, I never cease to be heartened by the endurance and affection of this bond, its strangeness, its apparent naturalness.

But fates are never quite aligned and our hearts so frequently broken. For many years I've had a news clipping on the pin-up board that overlooks my desk, a picture of a dog whose owner died in a tragic house-fire. There is something about the dog's hard-to-read gaze that I've always found compelling. It reminds me of many stories such as that of the famous Hachiko, the Japanese dog that waited patiently at Shibuya train station every evening, up to nine years after his owner, a university professor, had died suddenly at work. The sheer loyalty and urgent optimism of dogs has always been a great inspiration for their human companions, who so often wander from such virtuous paths and anxiously question their place in the world. No matter what future meets our planet, no matter how transformed or tragic, even apocalyptic, it's hard to imagine that a dog will not be there by our side, always urging us forward.

First published by Allen & Unwin in 2020

The original version of 'Dog' was published in *Tales From The Inner City*, Allen & Unwin 2018

Allen & Unwin
83 Alexander Street
Crows Nest NSW 2065
Australia
Phone: (61 2) 8425 0100
Email: info@allenandunwin.com
Web: www.allenandunwin.com

A catalogue record for this book is available from the National Library of Australia

ISBN 978 1 76052 613 9

For teaching resources, explore
www.allenandunwin.com/resources/for-teachers

Illustration technique: oil on canvas
Cover and text design by Shaun Tan
Set in 13 pt Gill Sans by Sandra Nobes
This book was printed in December 2024 by C&C Offset Printing Co. Ltd, China.

5 7 9 10 8 6 4